֍

In your heart live, big and small,

beings who do love you all:

giants, pixies—clever, sly—

elves and fairies in the sky.

Gnomes for certain will be there

kind and happy, do not despair.

Keep your beliefs forever alive,

they, and you, will surely thrive.

֍

Editor, English-language edition: Amy L. Vinchesi
Design Coordinator, English-language edition: Miko McGinty

ISBN 0-8109-4136-8

Originally published under the title *De Wereld van de kabouter*
Published in 1999 by Harry N. Abrams, Incorporated, New York
Printed and bound in Singapore

Harry N. Abrams, Inc.
100 Fifth Avenue
New York, N.Y. 10011
www.abramsbooks.com

Gnome Life

A
MONTHLY
CELEBRATION
OF
SECRETS,
TALES,
and
WHIMSY

❧

Wil Huygen

Illustrated by Rien Poortvliet

Harry N. Abrams, Inc., Publishers

JANUARY

Late at night, a thick layer of snow covers the ground and the tree branches. Snowflakes drift lightly from the sky, glistening softly between the stars. Their food hidden by the snow, the forest animals have nothing to eat. But atop a tree stump, in a small barn sticking out from the snow, Peter the Gnome has stored the acorns, nuts, and seeds he collected last fall. The barn is reached by a flight of stairs stretching from the ground to the tiny door. A squirrel has accidentally knocked off the bottom step, which is now missing, but Peter does not mind.

Hearing a muffled noise in the snowy night, Peter opens the door of his barn. Rabbit, Mouse, and Robin are outside, and they are hungry.

"Come little friends! Here are nuts and seeds for all of you," Peter calls. "Really, you ought to be sleeping. It is dark out, and you should all be in a warm bed. But I understand you were awakened by hunger."

Gnomes are only up and about at night. They sleep during the light of day, and this is why humans almost never see them. Peter does not sleep in the barn, for he has a cozy, warm house beneath the heavy roots of a nearby oak tree, with another store of food for his family.

When it is so dreadfully cold, Peter sits and waits for the animals inside the warm barn. He peeps through a slit in the door to see when they arrive. Many of them come very late at night, hoping for some food. During winter, many animals hibernate, or, to put it simply, they sleep indoors all season. Bats, lizards, snakes, badgers, and bears all hibernate. So do most beetles. Only in the spring, when the air and the earth's soil warm up, do these creatures' eyes begin to open, and their bodies wake from a long winter's nap.

Birds do not hibernate. Some prefer to leave home, and fly instead to a warm, sunny place far away, where they stay all winter. That's what we call migrating. In the spring, they return to make their nests. Those birds who stay in the forest throughout the winter sleep in the open air on a tree branch or on the ground, or sometimes in the eaves of a house.

Poor little birds have a hard time in the snow because they cannot find the seeds and bits of food they need. Fortunately, birds' feet do not freeze quite as quickly as ours do. Robin is able to stand in the snow for quite a while before his legs become cold. And at night, when he sleeps, he huddles his body down over his legs and then puffs up his feathers, turning himself into a little ball. This keeps him very warm.

Do the nuts and acorns in Peter's barn ever freeze? Yes, they do, because there is no stove in the barn. But it does not matter. They still taste good to the hungry animals.

You can help Peter and the other gnomes feed the birds in the winter by brushing away the snow from the ground and putting out some seeds or bread crumbs. Or, hang a birdfeeder outside your window so you can watch the birds come and go. Just remember to keep it filled with food!

Sadly, early comes the night
in a world so cold and white,
but know the watchful gnomes are there,
bringing food and tender care.

FEBRUARY

The severe cold lingers, as winter refuses to give way. A thick layer of snow covers everything, and the pond in the forest has frozen solid. Each night after feeding the hungry animals, Peter returns home from his little barn on the tree stump. Leif is Peter's son. He is twelve years old. He has a nice little pile of freshly made snowballs at his side. When Peter returns, Leif throws them at him. He strikes his father's right ear with one, making it turn a very deep red. But Peter does not mind. He just goes on his way, skiing on his handmade, wooden cross-country skis.

Another snowball whizzes by. "You'll have to aim better next time, my boy!"

Peter skis through the forest to see whether there are any animals in trouble who need his help. If the problem is serious, he does his best and then calls in the assistance of bigger animals, like foxes or pheasants or crows.

In the middle of the night, Peter comes home to share a nice big dinner with his wife Fern, Leif, and his daughter Lily. You now know that gnomes sleep during the daytime and are up all night—just the reverse of humans! After dinner, Peter brings out the sled that he made himself. The sled avoids thin spots in the ice and can move all on its own, thanks to the magical spell Peter has cast upon it.

Fern and the children jump into the sled, which travels at a great speed. Peter follows on his old-fashioned skates that were made by his great-grandfather from special wood found deep in the forest. They too are enchanted—you never get tired on them! The family travels far into the forest, faster and faster. Sometimes they visit other gnome families. Other times they collect things, like acorn caps, whittling wood, and special winter herbs and mosses.

Fern and Lily are under a warm blanket that Fern has made from sheep's wool and rabbit hair. Fern has an easy method for collecting wool. She just walks up to a sheep and says: "Good day, my dear sheep! May I have a bit of your nice wool?"

"Yeeees, byyyy all means," the sheep bleats in response. "Taaaake as much aaaas you like!"

"Thank you very much, dear sheep," Fern always says.

Or, she visits a rabbit hole. "Knock, knock," she calls. "May I enter?"

"Come in!" the rabbits reply. Fern walks into the rabbit hole. It is very dark, but gnomes can see exceedingly well in the dark.

The rabbits lounge comfortably in their warren, deep in the earth. There they have dug a nice home, where it is always dry and warm.

"May I have a bit of your fur?" Fern asks.

"Yes, certainly," the rabbits reply, "just pick it out of our coats."

So Fern combs their fur with a tiny fine-toothed comb, paying special attention to their soft white bellies and tails. The rabbits roll over onto their backs and enjoy it. They giggle and laugh. The hairs that collect in the comb Fern puts into a sack. When it is full, she thanks the rabbits and leaves the warren. Out of this fur and wool Fern makes thick socks, warm blankets, cozy vests and sweaters, and silky soft long underwear.

The pointed cap worn by the gnomes is made of felt. A fuzzy fabric, felt is produced from wool by beating, heating, and then pressing it. Gnomes never take off their caps. For the men and the boys the caps are red. Little girls wear green caps until they are grown up, and then they get a purple one.

Gnomes only have two children, and they are always the same age. This makes Leif and Lily . . . twins! Sometimes gnomes have two boys. Other times they have two girls. And sometimes, like Peter and Fern, they have a boy and a girl, like Leif and Lily.

If you look carefully, you will notice that the gnomes are not wearing mittens. That is because they can withstand the cold better than humans can. Gnomes do make mittens, but they hardly ever put them on. If Peter is really cold on long travels at night, he puts his hands under his beard to keep them warm.

Snow abounds in every place,
frosty winds blow in your face.
Spring still hovers far away,
and yet, it's lighter every day.

MARCH

Peter sits in his bath.

Actually, it is not a bath, since it has no spigots. It is a wooden tub. Peter made this one himself out of boards and two circular hoops to hold them together. It also has a wooden bottom. The boards fit together exactly so as not to let a single drop of water leak through. The tub is watertight.

Fern has filled the tub with bucket after bucket of hot water, which she has heated upon the stove. After that she puts in soap, which gnomes make out of a special soap herb. The soapy foam flows over the rim of the tub, but Peter will mop it up neatly afterwards.

After preparing the bath, Fern winds her wool, making a tight ball of it while Peter holds up the loops with his feet, which are sticking out of the sudsy tub. As he soaks Peter plays the flute. By the merry sounds of his music, Fern knows that the water is perfect, not too hot and not too cold.

Peter made the flute out of the roots of a nut tree. A flute made of nut wood has the finest sound. When outside Peter can use it to call others, since the sound travels for many miles.

On the floor behind the tub lies a long-handled brush. Peter scrubs his back with it, since with his hands he can only reach his bottom and his neck.

As soon as Fern has wound the wool into a ball, she starts to knit. For whom? For little Norah, the mouse. She sleeps in a basket. In a gnome house there are always a few pet mice.

They sleep in their basket in a corner of the living room, as dogs do in our homes. Lucy is Norah's sister. Fern has already knit a nice green sweater for her. Lucy looks into the mirror. She thinks herself very beautiful. She just cannot stop looking in the mirror.

Beyond the tub in the corner, a candle burns, held upright by a hand. But don't worry, it is not a real hand! It is made of wood. Peter has carved it out of a log of lime wood and attached it to the wall. The candle is made of beeswax. Gnomes have bee hives just like we do, but for a gnome a bee is a much larger creature in comparison. Thus they need only small portions of wax and honey, and the bees happily provide them.

A wooden basin with a carved head of a duck sits on the floor. It was made by Peter's grandfather, five hundred years ago. There is a washing glove in it.

When Peter climbs out of the tub, he dries himself off and dresses. He then goes outside to feed the birds and rabbits and mice, and any other friend who is hungry. This has to be done every evening.

When he gets home, Peter and Fern go to visit his old uncle, who has a terrible cold and is very grumpy because he is not able to go outside. Lily and Leif are staying with neighbors on the other side of the forest, so they will not be joining their parents. Peter and Fern are going to bring the uncle healing red currants, which contain a lot of vitamin C, from their cool, damp room beneath the house, where currants and other fruits and vegetables remain fresh all winter.

Fern has put on a special purple cap and her nicest clothes.

"How beautiful you are!" Peter says. "I'm going to kiss you!"

"Enough of that!" Fern says, blushing. "It's time to leave!"

"We have to watch out for falling fir apples!" Peter says.

And so, kissing the mice on their noses and locking up the house, they set out. A little wren joins Peter and Fern, just to enjoy their company.

And, to help watch out for falling fir apples!

Warm and deep beneath the earth

live the gnomes their daily life,

always full of contented mirth,

man and twins and faithful wife.

APRIL

Springtime is right around the corner, and buds begin to bloom on all the trees and shrubs. They grow fatter and fatter until they finally burst open, and then out come small, bright green leaves. If you observe the forest from a distance, you can see a greenish haze over every living thing. The gnomes feel great joy because everything is so green and new.

Peter is about to embark upon a journey. Somewhere far away, in another land, a small child is ill, and Peter will make the little one healthy again. All gnomes have some medical skills by nature, but Peter is a real doctor. He has studied medicine with very old and learned gnome professors, and he knows all about herbs

and remedies for many different kinds of illness.

"Do you have pain in your little tummy?" he may inquire. "If so, you must drink this tea."

Or, he asks, "Do you have a toothache? Then you should smear it with this oil!"

In order to travel to the child faster, Peter rides on the backs of a female duck and her husband, the drake. During the journey, the ducks switch Peter back and forth when the other gets tired. You see, a gnome weighs three hundred grams, which is the same as ten and one half ounces, and this can be a lot for the ducks to carry on their backs. But they are happy to help, because Peter is very good company.

You can tell the difference between the female duck and the drake by their feathers. Hers are almost totally brown, while the drake has an iridescent, greenish head and neck, which shine like polished shoes when the sun is out.

Fern, Lily, and Leif stand on a piece of dead tree between the reeds at the water's edge, the easiest spot from which to step onto the back of the duck. They wave to Peter and the ducks as they begin their flight.

The ducks had already begun to nest, as ducks do in April. When it is a mild winter they actually start in March. The female duck lays one egg in her nest each day, until she has thirteen. This duck has already laid three eggs.

If she must leave the nest alone for a while, the duck first hides her eggs from the crows and magpies by covering the nest with dry grass and lots of small down feathers. This works most of the time, but other times the nest is seen and then destroyed by these predators, who peck the eggs open and eat their contents. Then the mother duck must start a brand-new nest somewhere else.

This duck is expecting to lay her fourth egg early tomorrow morning. But in the meantime she easily can bring Peter to the sick child.

"Bye-bye, my love!" Fern calls. "Take good care of yourself!"

"I will, I will!" Peter shouts as he waves his hand.

"Quack, quack," cries the female duck. She always quacks during takeoff, while the drake makes soft little squeaking sounds.

But only gnomes understand what they say. And other ducks, of course.

Are you perhaps the finest bride
with all your greenish splendor,
you must be oh so full of pride
with buds and leaves so tender.

MAY

In the very early morning, the forest is wet with dew. Every blade of grass is studded with droplets, which sparkle in the sun like diamonds. There are many colorful blossoms this May, and newly hatched young birds perch wobbly in the trees. Their parents are very busy finding them food, because they are hungry all the time and cannot yet feed themselves. In the meantime, Fern and Peter provide the young birds with small seeds left over from the food stored for last winter in the little barn on the tree stump.

Two birds have already had some flying lessons and have just left their nest. They have not exactly flown, though—their skill and strength are only enough to let them flutter carefully from branch to branch. In a few more weeks the birds will be able to glide smoothly through the air, but right now they are still quite helpless, keeping their beaks wide open and chirping in anticipation of food.

Peter has made a tiny gnome ladder to help Fern reach the birds. Some day, if you are lucky, you might actually see one of these ladders standing in the woods. But if you do, you must be very, very quiet. You should always be quiet in the forest, for if you shout or rustle the bushes, you will scare away all the gnomes and animals.

Peter perches on the head of a young buck to get as close as possible to the small bird.

The buck is far too tall for Peter to mount by himself. So the animal must lie down on the ground first, allowing Peter to climb onto its back. Then the buck stands up and Peter scurries up onto his head.

How do you know this is a buck, or a male deer? Because he has a set of antlers on his head. Female deer, or does, do not have any antlers. What exactly are antlers? Well, they are made of two hard boughs of ribbed bone, which are very strong and almost unbreakable. They grow branches, just like a tree, that end in sharp points. Bucks use their antlers to fight other bucks during mating season.

From his perch, Peter at first cannot reach all the way to the bird's open beak, and so he asks the deer, "Would you bend your beautiful head a little lower, brother buck?"

The buck bows deeper until Peter is able to give the bird some seeds.

"Here you are. Enjoy this seed!" Peter says. "You must eat to grow big and strong!"

Peter and Fern have to stay with the birds until their parents return, since they are too young to recognize the danger of a hawk or an eagle, who might grab and eat them.

When a hawk does dive down suddenly to snatch one, Peter puts up his hand like a policeman. "Oh no, brother hawk!" He says calmly. "You will not get these little birds! I am the boss here!"

And so the hawk retreats, because all animals obey the gnomes. As soon as the baby birds' parents return, Peter and Fern go home, and with their children go right to bed.

When walking through the woods and fields you can sometimes spot a deer, and, if you are lucky, three or four together. In the summertime, the deer are orangish-red in hue, and in the winter they are greyish-brown. But you must be there early in the morning or just before darkness descends in the evening. And whenever you go, you must be very, very quiet.

Early morning in the wood,

gnomes and deer are still afoot,

birdsongs warble in your ear,

far and wide the air is clear.

JUNE

Peter sits on his swing. Norah, one of the two pet mice, sits with him. Peter loves to swing, usually quietly by himself, because it helps him think. He has much to think about, as everybody asks his advice, sometimes in very difficult matters. If Peter swings lightly, without much effort, he feels peaceful and calm, and it is then that the best thoughts come to him.

But today Peter knows no peace. Norah wants to swing fast and high. When Norah was younger, she was scared and would not even sit on the swing. But now she loves it. Now it cannot go too high for her.

"Higher, higher!" she squeaks, swishing her tail in pleasure. She is too small to hold onto both ropes at once, so with her left paw she holds onto Peter. He made the swing himself. Gnomes make *everything* themselves. If they ever need

help, they call on another gnome, or two or three if need be.

When Peter and Norah have finished swinging, Peter and Fern decide to go for a walk around the forest pond. There they meet a frog.

"Hello Peter! Hello Fern!" the frog croaks. "Do you, by any chance, have a rope with you?"

Peter always carries a rope in his pouch, but he asks innocently, "A rope? What would you like a rope for?"

"To go skipping of course!" answers the frog.

"Well, let's skip then!" Peter says. With a wink to Fern, he gives her one end of the rope. As they swing it between them, the frog skips over the rope, going faster and faster. Frogs never get tangled in jump ropes, because they never let them get caught between their feet—they are too good at jumping for that! At times the frog gets so wild, he leaps all the way over Fern's head!

"Have you had enough yet?" Peter asks, hopefully.

"No, no!" the frog shouts. "More, more!"

Peter sighs but again winks at Fern. "Please sing your jumping song, Fern."

And Fern sings to the beat of the swinging rope:

> What time is it? It's twelve o'clock.
> Who says so? Old Fritz.
> Where is he? In the cellar.
> What's he do? He knits.
> Old Fritz, he knits.
> For whom, for whom?
> For little Boom-Boom,
> for big Bim-Bam,
> for old Sim-Sam!

"That's it. Enough for today!" Peter says, putting away the rope.

"Thank you very much!" croaks the frog, and disappears with a mighty jump into the pond.

The jump-roping frog was a green frog. They stay mainly in their own ponds, croaking loudly, over and over again, especially when they are trying to attract a female frog. There are also brown frogs, with just a little bit of green showing on their backs. These frogs migrate from pond to pond, chasing out the green frogs. It is a pity that there are not many green frogs to be found these days, so if you do see one, you know that you have to be very careful with it. Just as you have to be very careful with everything in nature.

On a velvet night in June,

when there is a round full moon,

gleeful dancing gnomes abound,

blowing flutes with merry sound.

Atop a mushroom stands a cake,

a sugary slice for each to take.

Bride and bridegroom dance together,

in her hair she wears a feather.

JULY

It's time for Peter to teach his children about mushrooms. You see, there are many different kinds, and some of them are poisonous! In the summer and fall, mushrooms grow in the woods and fields. The gnomes can tell the good ones from the bad, but even they have to learn the differences when they are young. Leif, Lily, Lucy, and Fern listen carefully to Peter, who begins the lesson earnestly.

"Listen well! In a few weeks, mushrooms will be growing everywhere, and you will have to know which ones you can eat and which ones you cannot. Mushrooms are good food, full of protein, and protein is something you need for a strong, healthy body. Meat, fish, milk, and eggs also contain protein. Since we gnomes do not eat meat or fish, we eat mushrooms instead, along with eggs and milk, but only if the animals give them to us.

"But some mushrooms are poisonous! If you eat them, you can get very sick and even die. On the other side of this chart are pictures of both poisonous and nonpoisonous mushrooms, and you must learn their appearance by heart. Look closely, and study this chart over and over again."

Fern sits with her children, even though she has known the mushrooms by heart since her early youth (she is now close to one hundred years old!). But she likes to listen to Peter's lesson time and again. After all, you cannot be too careful with mushrooms.

"Mind you," Peter says. "For now you are only allowed to go *searching* for mushrooms with Mother or me. Never eat or put in your mouth *anything* you find outdoors!"

The children nod. Lily puts her arm around Lucy's warm little mouse body, who in turn snuggles up to her cozily. Lucy cannot read the chart though, so it is a relief that she does not like mushrooms.

Behind the chart is a big oak tree, under whose roots lies the gnome house where Peter, Fern, Leif, Lily, and the mice live. The house has only one window, above the ground, which looks into the attic. Inside, in the parlor and in other parts of the house, candles are burning. When he built the house, Peter covered the exterior of the attic with oak bark so it would look just like a part of the tree.

Where is Norah? Ah, Lucy's sister mouse is asleep again in her basket downstairs. She sleeps soundly, at all hours of the day and night. Peter teases her now and then. "You are sleeping just like a dormouse, Norah. Are you, by any chance, a dormouse?"

"No, I am not a dormouse." Norah says, peevishly. "A dormouse sleeps for seventeen hours each day, and I sleep only thirteen!"

And then they all laugh, except Norah, who just does not find it funny.

Buzzing go the busy bees,

from fruit to fruit upon the trees.

What dessert might each gnome please?

Sugar, cream, and blackberries!

AUGUST

In the early morning, after a very hot night, Peter reads aloud from the Secret Book before going to bed. He has been working all night, filling up his store houses with fruit. When autumn comes, he will finish the job by adding nuts and acorns. A tawny owl and a sparrow listen in.

Do you know what the Secret Book is? I'll tell you. Every gnome has a copy in his or her house. It actually consists of seven books, one of which Peter now holds in his lap. In these mysterious volumes, everything that gnomes know is written down, including gnome fairy tales. Peter reads one of them to his friends. Perched on a purple thistle is a butterfly, but she is far too busy to listen to the tale. Instead, she eagerly drinks with her long, narrow tongue all the thistle's sweet honey.

The owl and the sparrow love to listen to Peter's tales. Owls are very learned, though not as learned as a gnome, naturally. But they are very wise and understand a great deal. The sparrow looks as if he too is learned, but he honestly does not know very much. Sparrows usually live in towns, but this bird is an old friend of Peter's, and he has come into the woods to visit him.

When Peter finishes the fairy tale, the owl loudly snaps his beak and the sparrow chirps sweetly, thanking Peter and telling him how beautifully his story was told. In fact, they want him to continue.

"My dear fellow," coos the owl. "Would you . . . oo oo . . . be so good . . . oo oo . . . as to read another fairy tale, just one?"

"Yes, yes, hurrah!" chirps the sparrow. "Another one, another one!"

"Well, all right, but just one more," Peter sighs, for he is very tired and the air is getting very hot again.

"A tale for naughty children," he begins. "It goes like this: Once upon a time, in a wide creek in the meadow, there was a little frog. He was a disobedient frog. He always went too far from home.

"One day his mother said to him 'Beware of the stork, little one. If you see two red sticks standing in the water, you must get away as quickly as you can, for those sticks are really the legs of a stork who is waiting to catch and eat you!'

"But one day, as usual, the little frog swam too far from home. Suddenly he came upon one shiny red stick standing in the water.

"'Well, that will do no harm,' the little frog thought to himself. 'It is only one stick!'

"But it was a stork all right, standing up on one leg. (Storks like to do that.) And so the little frog swam by the red stick as if nothing was the matter.

"Swish! The stork swooped down and—snap!—plucked the frog from the water by his leg. Fortunately, however, he couldn't get a proper hold because the leg was too slippery. So, with a twist and then a tug, the little frog tore himself loose, losing only his big toe inside the stork's tight beak. Hitting the water with a splash, the frog dove as deep as he could, swimming to safety under the cover of the water plants.

"When he got home his mother put him to bed and called upon the gnomes to nurse his left foot, now missing a big toe. He stayed in bed this way for two weeks! But, after that, he was again able to jump and swim. He would limp a little bit though, provoking other frogs to shout when they saw him: 'Froggy, froggy mind your feet, there's a stork here in the reed!'

"And the little frog would dive deep and quickly swim away, for he had promised both his mother and himself to steer clear of storks for the rest of his life!"

August is the harvest time,

crops are ripe and in their prime.

Using every scrap of light,

farmers work till late at night.

As the summer takes its leave,

every gnome will now retrieve

all the fruits he can obtain

for the cold times once again.

SEPTEMBER

With autumn comes berry-picking season, and the blackberries have just become ripe, turning a dark blue, or even a black hue. They taste very sweet. The berries grow on big brambles with shaggy thorns, and some parts of the forest are filled with them. Brambles are excellent hiding places for small animals like rabbits, lizards, pheasants, and partridges, for the hawks and the crows cannot attack them through the thorns and tangled branches. Foxes detest brambles, too, for this very reason.

Blackberries are simple fruits. They grow independently, needing only the sun, the rain, and the soil—nobody else needs to do a thing for them. Peter picks the plump, ripe blackberries from the bramble, carefully watching out for the thorns, though he hardly ever pricks himself. Each fat blackberry he collects gets tossed down to Leif and Lily, who wait eagerly to grab them with open arms.

"There you are, Leif! Look out, Lily!" Peter calls out repeatedly. "Catch it now!"

The children catch the blackberries cleanly, and then give them to their mother. Fern places them in neat piles in the pushcart, putting bramble leaflets in between to keep the blackberries fresh. There are no thorns on the leaflets because they grow only on the bramble stems.

Do you know why blackberries are so plentiful and unspoiled within the brambles? It is because the birds cannot get to them. Though they would love to eat the berries, they would hurt their legs and feet if they landed on a bramble branch. So to avoid injury, the birds leave the blackberries for the gnomes to gather. The berries are not always their beautiful blue-black hue—if you look carefully into a blackberry bramble, you will usually also see red, unripened blackberries bunched around the darker ones.

Blackberries are a wholesome food, containing a lot of vitamin C. Out of the blackberries gathered from the bramble Fern makes jam, or jelly, or juice, or a blackberry cake. Or, she simply serves them on a plate with sugar.

And what of that creature there beneath the handles of the cart? Well, it is a snail. These small creatures have a soft, fleshy body and a hard shell. The shell is a snail's house, and he carries it on his back with him everywhere. In times of danger, or when turning in for the night, the snail pulls his whole body into his little house. Those two things that look like sticks on the top of his head are feelers. With them the snail can sense whether or not things are safe on the path in front of him. This is very helpful, because his eyes are located just in front of the feelers, at their base.

A snail is always wet and slimy. If it dries out, a snail dies. Therefore, they like to slither around in wet grass or on wet leaves. If the weather is very warm and dry, snails creep away to a cool, dark spot, withdraw into their little houses, and then wait patiently until the rain returns, or until there is abundant dew on the grass.

Peter uses a woven basket with a strap to collect the highest blackberries on the bush, which are too high to be safely thrown to the children. Instead, Peter climbs up to the berries and then carefully places them in his shoulder basket. This way, when he comes down the ladder he will not squash the berries—or Fern or Leif or Lily!

Magpie, magpie, flutter and flee,

turn up your tail and grant good luck to me,

one for sorrow, two for joy,

three for a girl, and four for a boy,

five for silver, six for gold,

seven for a secret never to be told!

OCTOBER

In October, the days become shorter, evening darkness settles sooner, and the morning sun rises even later. The leaves on the trees turn from green to vibrant yellows, oranges, and reds, before drifting softly from the branches onto the ground.

Peter has come home from a long night's journey, and the children have already gone to bed. But before Peter turns in, he first plays a game of shuffleboard with Fern, keeping score on a small piece of paper.

An insect drops into the room and starts crawling over the partitions of the shuffleboard. Since it is October, clearly the winged bug must be looking for a cozy place to hibernate, and landed in the gnome house by accident.

"Out of the way, please, little bug!" Fern says. "Otherwise you will be whacked in the leg by a shuffle disk!"

"Just pick him up and drop him outside the front door," Peter suggests. "He will surely find a nice hibernation spot to crawl into."

This bug appears to have four wings, but the brown ones are actually wing sheaths. They are hard and shiny and water cannot get through them. The bug flies through the air by flapping his white wings, and when he wants to take a rest and just crawl for a while, the bug neatly folds up his white wings and slips the wing

sheaths very carefully over them, protecting them from the rain and against injury.

Because Fern shooed the little bug off the shuffleboard, he unfolds his sheaths and wings and prepares to fly away. But this is not necessary, as Fern will carefully pick him up and put him outside the door.

The fire inside the stove behind Peter is low because the gnomes have finished their dinner already. Upon the stove Fern heats a warm broth that gnomes like to drink before bedtime—it gives them pleasant dreams!

The sun is about to rise, but its rays do not reach the gnome house, deep under the roots of the oak tree. This does not bother Peter and his family though, as gnomes do not need to see the sun to know exactly what is going on outside— they are one with nature.

Peter and Fern prepare for bed, keeping their pointed caps on all the while, as gnomes are supposed to. No one has ever seen a gnome without his or her cap. Peter does pull off his thick woolen socks, though.

"I am ready for a long day's sleep!" he says, winking. Once in bed in their sleeping cupboard, Peter snores loudly, but Fern is used to it. Sometimes, without Peter noticing, she puts a wad of wool in each of her ears.

Golden hazes over plains,

freshest smells just after rains.

Mushrooms sprout in many spots,

time to bring in the flowerpots.

NOVEMBER

Peter sleeps soundly in his easy chair one early morning after coming in from a long night's work. Fern and the children are still awake, but Peter was so tired that he didn't even light his pipe. What was it that he worked so hard on? I'll tell you.

There was a large hollow tree in the wood, tall enough to easily fit three men standing on each other's shoulders. Thirty-three bats had just started their deep winter sleep inside the tree, hanging upside down by the long claws on their hind legs, when the gnomes learned that it was to be cut down by lumberjacks.

If that happened, the bats would wake up too early and then they would die. You see, once disturbed from their hibernation, bats have to

eat within a few days—any kind of flying insect will do—but that is impossible in November, a time when there are no insects. The bats can live for a short time on fat stored in their tiny bodies, but this would never last until Spring.

Peter and several other gnomes rescued the bats so carefully that not one of them even woke up. First they tenderly lifted them from their perch within the tree and quietly placed them in baskets. These they then hung around the neck of some friendly geese, who carried the bats through the night to another forest.

After three trips, all accompanied by Peter, the gnomes very carefully hung the bats in a new hollow tree, where they will sleep comfortably through the winter. There are no plans to cut down this tree, at least not yet. Remember— trees are a sacred part of the earth and we must respect them as such.

So after this adventure, Peter falls fast asleep in his chair. Fern sets the table for dinner, the plates in a neat stack on the floor. Leif is naughty, tossing rings around his father's pointed cap, but his mother gently scolds him.

Outside the wind howls, the rain comes down in sheets, and the forest will be frozen within a few days. But here, in the gnome home under the roots of the heavy oak tree, it is safe, warm, and dry.

In the vast and lonely woods
gnomes prepare their winter goods:
clothing, food, and snowproof boots.
Nature is now crisp and fair,
watch that forest over there—

just before they're turning bare,
trees display a colored scene,
yellow, red, and brownish-green,
worthy for a fairy queen.

DECEMBER

The fifth of December is the most exciting night of the year for gnome children. Santa Claus comes down the chimney with his golden staff, bringing gaily wrapped presents for all the good little children. Black Ben, the mole, is Santa's helper. He wears a yellow velvet cap with a bluejay's feather stuck in it, and he carries Santa's sack.

The gnome Santa Claus and Black Ben have squeezed through Peter and Fern's chimney, but Peter is not at home—he had something urgent to do elsewhere!

"Well, Fern," Santa Claus asks, in his booming voice. "Have Lily and Leif been good, honest children?"

"Oh yes, Santa," Fern says. "Apart from the usual playful naughtiness!"

"What kind of naughtiness?" Santa Claus demands.

Leif and Lily are timid and silent.

"Come, come!" Santa Claus says. "What have they done?"

But Leif and Lily can only stare with wide, frightened eyes at Santa Claus and Ben.

"Black Ben," Santa Claus says, "do you know by any chance whether these children have done naughty things?"

"Well, Santa Claus," Ben squeaks, "I did hear that Lily teased her brother, and once even her mother! And I know that Leif does at times throw rings around his father's cap when the poor man is taking a nap."

"Oh, ho, ho," Santa Claus rumbles. "Teasing her brother, and throwing rings around the cap of his father!"

"And," Ben continues, "I have been told too of Leif flying a bumble bee as a kite after putting a rope around one of his legs!"

"Good heavens," Santa Claus cries. "Poor insect!"

"But for the most part they have been good and honest, Santa Claus," Ben admitted. "Lily always helps her mother set the table, wash the dishes, and make the beds, and Leif cuts wood and does his chores in the garden!"

"And do they read diligently from the Secret Book?"

"Yes, Santa Claus. They read the Secret Book every day, and they are both excellent readers, as young as they are!"

"Very well," Santa Claus says. "Come on, Black Ben, have a look in your sack. Perhaps there are some presents left for these sweet little children!"

With his big clumsy claws, Ben digs in the sack, hindered only slightly by his lace pleated collar, and produces some wonderful gifts. For Lily there are new knitting needles, a little handbag, books, and delicious chocolates. And for Leif there is a croquet set, a magic rope, a knife for whittling, and a puzzle.

"Ho-ho-ho!" Santa Claus says gleefully. "We must go on to the next chimney, and look for other good children. Goodbye, Leif, goodbye, Lily, goodbye, Fern!"

"Have a good journey, Santa Claus!" Fern calls. "And thank you very much for coming. I hope you will be back next year. Come on, children, say something!"

"Goodbye, Santa Claus," Leif says very softly. Fern gently prods them again: "Say thank you…."

"Thank you very much, Santa Claus!" the children chime in unison.

And so, holiday joy settles around the gnome home, as Leif and Lily play with their new toys and eagerly wait for Peter to return. Where has he been and whom has he helped tonight?

Pale and meager seems the sun;

inside the house is all the fun.

Santa Claus and Christmas days

surround the hearth with logs ablaze.